THE ORIGINAL MEDITERRANEAN DIET COOKBOOK FOR BEGINNERS

Healthy and Delicious Meals for Every Day incl. 28-Day Meal Plan

Tony A. Morgan

TABLE OF CONTENTS

WHAT IS THE MEDITERRANEAN DIET?

The Mediterranean diet is among the most popular diets currently. The major reason for its popularity is that it was voted by a majority as among the best diets of 2019. While this is impressive, the diet comes with a myriad of health benefits that has a lot of people around the globe jumping to this train that is just taking off.

The diet is linked with benefits including weight loss, improved brain functions, and overall heart health. Even more, fascinating about this diet is that it a lifestyle. This diet incorporates the selection of meals and preparation taking after how it is done originally.

If you have tried researching the diet before, then you will agree with me that there is no definitive definition or approach to this diet. While we acknowledge this, this recipe book, therefore, serves as a guide that will bring you up to speed on all the ways you can fully tap into the benefits of this diet.

Let's dive in!

WHY THE MEDITERRANEAN DIET?

To begin, the whole idea that brought the diet to light was that the Mediterranean regions suffered the least when coronary heart problems are concerned. Mediterranean countries, for instance, Italy, Greece, and Crete had less heart disease fatalities as compared to countries like the US or northern Europe. More research on the likely cause directly linked the diet from the Mediterranean region as the contributing factor. You will be impressed to know that the Mediterranean diet is fully endorsed by UNESCO as a sustainable and healthy dietary plan you can heavily benefit from. This dietary plan has its building blocks from traditional meals and fruits often prepared using simple cooking methods that are friendly to the heart.

WHAT IS THE MEDITERRANEAN DIET COMPOSED OF?

As described earlier, there is no one single approach to this diet that is followed by everyone. However, there are some fundamental guidelines and approaches that you can follow including the following:

- ✓ Daily intake of healthy fats, veggies, fruits, and whole grains.
- ✓ Weekly consumption of fish, eggs, poultry, and beans.
- ✓ Reduced consumption of red meat.
- ✓ A reasonable amount of dairy products.

Other than the above, other inclusions might not apply to everyone, for instance, taking a glass of wine after meals. The Mediterranean lifestyle also includes sharing meals with family for mental benefits it comes along with.

Healthy fats

This diet plan involves the use of healthy fats as an alternative to saturated fats which is not good for the heart. One primary sauce of healthy fats is olive oil. Olive oil is central to this diet thanks to its heart-friendly nature. It functions by providing monosaturated fats which lower the overall cholesterol level in the body. Other than olive oil, seeds and nuts are also essential to this diet. The same goes for fatty fishes, for example, sardines and lake trout.

Wine

The inclusion of wine among recipes is a gray area because people have varied opinions about wine. However, most of the Mediterranean dietary plans provide for the inclusion of wine after meals in moderation. As for the American guidelines, consumption of wine in moderation is also accepted. So as far as the inclusion of wine in the diet, the best approach is weighing the benefits and the risk and deciding as an individual if it is best to include as part of your diet.

IS IT WORTH ALL THE BUZZ?

It is worth mentioning that the Mediterranean diet was among the top 10 best diets for weight loss. While it is not inclined to weight loss, this diet is enjoyed by many because it is the least restrictive diet you can try. The Mediterranean diet is a holistic diet composed of healthy foods that provide overall health to your body. This is the reason why people in the Mediterranean regions live longer as compared to any other regions in the world. The selection of foods to eat and the methods of preparation are the whole idea of this diet which is now becoming a lifestyle.

WHAT ARE THE HEALTH BENEFITS OF THE MEDITERRANEAN DIET?

Preventing heart diseases and stroke

This should not be surprising in any way. The Mediterranean diet restricts the intake of processed foods, red meat, refined slices of bread, and encourages the drinking of red wine in moderation instead of downing cups of hard liquor. These are all factors that can reduce the risk of you developing a stroke and also heart diseases.

Reducing the risk of Alzheimer's

Research conducted into unraveling the benefits of Mediterranean diets has revealed that it helps to improve blood sugar levels, cholesterol, and maintain optimum blood vessel health. Which in turn keeps you clear of Alzheimer's.

Reducing the risk of Parkinson's disease

The high proportion of antioxidants in Mediterranean diets, gotten from the high proportion of vegetables, and fruits helps to prevent cells from undergoing the process of oxidative stress. This cuts the risk of developing Parkinson's disease in half.

For agility

Coupled with the physical activity advised as an integral of the Mediterranean diet, if you are an older individual, the nutrients derived from the diet goes a long way in reducing the risk of you developing muscle weakness and other obvious signs of frailty by as far as 70%.

Protection against type 2 diabetes

This may come as a surprise since there is the general mythical knowledge that any diet rich in sugar or sugar-like items such as the wine regarded as an integral of this diet, amongst other things cannot be seen to help in protection against type 2 diabetes.

However, this is an exception. The Mediterranean diet is very rich in fiber and digests slowly. It helps to prevent swings in blood sugar and also goes a long way in maintaining a healthy weight.

SHORTCOMING OF THE DIET

Milk

The only significant shortcoming to this diet is the limitation on the consumption of milk. If you depend on milk as the primary source of your calcium, then you will need to get an alternative. Stick to cheese and skim milk as alternatives

Cooking time

If you decide to choose the Mediterranean diet as your diet plan, then you should have no problem getting in the kitchen to prepare meals. In fact, the constant need for fresh food frequently will mean that you will have to spend more hours in the kitchen than you have before.

IS THE MEDITERRANEAN DIET EXPENSIVE?

The overall cost of the diet is entirely dependent on your consumption as an individual. Also, the cost will be determined by how you choose to shape your recipes. It is common knowledge that some of the ingredients might be expensive in some places so expect a small difference when comparing to the ingredients you are using. However, if you are moving away from red meat to a plant-based Mediterranean diet, you are diet plan is likely to cost less than before. Some veggies are expensive than others, with this diet, you are free to choose whatever veggie that is within your purchasing power.

WHAT YOU SHOULD EAT
WHILE ON THIS DIET

Salmon

Including the salmon on your meal plans is very necessary while on this diet plan. Salmons are good sources of healthy fats and also omega 2 fatty acids which are healthy for your body. In fact, the American Heart association reckons that you should have at least 2 fish containing meals per week, and salmon is a good choice.

Olive oil

One of the major differences the diet has when compared to other meal plans is the fact that it has replaced foods high in saturated fats like butter with plant sources rich in monounsaturated fatty; acids, an example being olive oil.

Chickpeas

The main nutrition in chickpeas, hummus contains a sizable amount of fiber, coupled with lots of zinc, iron, folate, and magnesium. Which according to a paper published in November 2014 in the Journal of applied nutrition, metabolism and physiology. The statistics available are for a whole cup and you only need just half a cup to reap the benefits.

Pomegranates

This fruit is also one that is packed full of antioxidants and anti-inflammatory components. This fruit has also been linked to cancer prevention in some cases; since it contains some anti-cancer properties. This is according to research published in the Journal of Advanced Biomedical Research in the year 2014.

Greek yogurt

This is also another staple of the Mediterranean diet. Dairy components of the diet need to be consumed in moderate amounts. As a result, opting for Greek yogurt is ideal since it is a source of low or non-saturated fat food.

Arugula

The leafy green veggies such as the arugula are consumed in abundance in this diet. The meal plan entails eating green veggies more times than normal therefore reducing the chances of developing Alzheimer's significantly.

Farro

As mentioned earlier, whole grains are an integral part of the Mediterranean diet. This delightful grain meal offers a satisfying source of protein and fiber. Not only are cereals a source of fiber, but also help in the prevention of diseases like cancer and also diabetes.

AVOID THESE FOODS WHEN ON THE DIET

Red meat

The Mediterranean diet as a whole is not big on red meat. And its consumption in large amounts is not advised. The meal plan has a vegetarian angle to it and it mostly makes use of animal protein as only a compliment and not as the main dish.

Refined sugars

Aside from refined sugars and all its attendant side effects, it is also not accepted as part of the Mediterranean diet. The meal plan does not require the use of lots of sugars, so instead, it is advised that a beginner or one starting on the diet should avoid sugar and anything of that nature. This includes most baked foods and syrup-sweetened drinks like artificial juices and soda.

If you have a sweet tooth, it is advisable to turn to honey, fruits, or baked foods made with natural sweeteners like honey and cinnamon to get your fix.

Hard liquor

This must have been mentioned at one point or the other. As far as the Mediterranean diet is concerned, hard liquors such as tequila and Vodka are not allowed. If you are one that drinks alcohol consistently, you might need to stick to red wine as opposed to hard liquors.

IS THE MEDITERRANEAN DIET GOOD FOR WEIGHT LOSS?

There is always the fear that consuming foods rich in fat will always lead to an accumulation of fat. While there is some truth to this fear, it is also worth mentioning that a caloric surplus is the only cause of accumulation of fat in the body. So, the Mediterranean diet can also be tweaked to steer you towards weight loss. The best approach to this is by building a Mediterranean meal plan that will ensure you are always on a caloric deficit. To help with the deficit, you should engage in physical exercise to burn off extra calories.

HOW TO GET STARTED WITH THE DIET

Before getting used to the Mediterranean diet or lifestyle, you will have some adapting to do. One thing that you should always keep in mind is that this diet leaves room for experimentation with the recipes thanks to the myriad of ingredients.

It is wise to plan your meals beforehand. As a beginner, you don't need to shop for everything at once, you may start with the simple recipes and shop for more as your recipes advance to the next level.

Remember, the Mediterranean diet is a lifelong process that you should learn to stick to, unlike other short-term diets. This diet is the way to go if you are to change your life for the better, this new diet plan will not only ensure that you are healthy but also enjoy tasty meals without necessarily having to starve yourself.

Start with the easy recipes as a beginner and you will incorporate new ones along the way, over time, you will also learn how to balance your portions to ensure a caloric deficit if you are looking to lose weight

Mediterranean Breakfast Recipes

The Mediterranean Easy ShakShuka

Time: 35 minutes | Servings 4
Kcal 331, Carbs 21.6g/0.76oz, Fats 22.2g/0.78oz, Proteins 15.7g/0.55oz, Fiber 5.9oz/0.2oz

Ingredients

- 60g/4 tablespoons of Sriracha
- 60g/¼ cup of Greek yogurt (plain)
- 450g/16oz firm tofu
- 60g/¼ a cup of mayonnaise
- 30ml/2 tablespoons; soy sauce

- 600g/5 cups of broccoli (chopped)
- 15ml/1 tablespoon of vegetable oil
- A clove of garlic minced
- 15ml/1 tablespoon of sesame oil

For the Cauliflower stir rice

- 2ml/½ a teaspoon of sesame oil (toasted)
- ½ a cauliflower head
- 30ml/2 tablespoons of soy sauce
- 15ml/2 tablespoons olive oil
- 2 whole eggs
- ½ a cup chopped white onions
- 75g/½ a cup of frozen peas
- 2 minced garlic cloves
- 2 diced large carrots

Preparation

1. For the cauliflower stir rice, begin by chopping down the cauliflower to manageable florets before blitzing using any food processor till reduced to rice-like size.

2. Bring the olive oil to heat over medium temperatures before putting in the chopped veggies. Cook until tender.

3. Once cooked, create a circular hole between the veggies and crack the two eggs right at the center. Allow the eggs to scramble completely before stirring together with the veggies. Drizzle atop with some olive and sesame oils.

4. For the tofu, start by squeezing as much moisture as possible using your hands.

5. Chop into smaller pieces before adding them into a medium skillet then put in the vegetable oil, garlic, and sesame oil.

6. Allow cooking over high to medium heat till nice and crispy.

7. In a small microwaveable bowl, put in the broccoli before adding in a little water.

8. Using a suitable cover, i.e. plastic wrap, cover the bowl before cooking in the microwave till tender and bright green.

9. Now mix the mayo, Sriracha, and yogurt to a consistent paste.

10. Add a spoonful of the sauce into 5 mason jars. Into each jar, top with some rice, veggies, and tofu in that order.

11. You can keep in the refrigerator for up to a maximum of 5 days. Be sure to microwave before serving.

Breakfast Hash with Sweet Potatoes and Brussel Sprouts

Time: 35 minutes | Servings 4
Kcal 206, Carbs 19.3g/0.68oz, Fats 9.7g/0,34oz, Proteins 11g/0.39oz, Fiber 4.8g/0.17oz

Ingredients

Brussel sprouts and sweet potatoes

- A pinch of salt
- 1 large sweet potato chopped into bite-size
- A pinch of black pepper
- 360g/3 cups of ¼ Brussel sprouts
- 15ml/1 tablespoon of avocado oil

For the rest

- 4 large eggs
- 30ml/2 tablespoon of avocado oil
- 2 cups of freshly chopped spinach
- ½ medium red, white, and yellow chopped onions
- 120g/1 cup of spicy chicken or pork sausage
- 3 minced garlic cloves
- 34g/2 tablespoons of dried currants
- 90g/¾ a cup of dried fuji (finely diced)
- 17g/1 tablespoon of minced sage

For serving

- Fresh parsley

Preparation

1. Bring the oven to a temperature of 204°C/400°F then spread a parchment pepper at the bottom of a baking dish.

2. Put the Brussel sprouts and sweet potatoes in the baking dish. Sprinkle some salt and pepper atop then mix well.

3. Allow cooking for 25 minutes till golden brown. Remember to flip and toss halfway through.

4. Meanwhile, bring a large skillet to heat over medium temperatures.

5. Add in some oil and the onions. Quickly sauté for a minute then add in the currants, garlic, diced fuji, and sage.

6. Cook for 3 minutes till nice and fragrant.

7. Now throw in the sausages, stir, and allow cooking till the sausages are nice and cooked through. Be sure to stir often while breaking the sausages into small chunks using a spoon.

8. Once cooked, stir in the spinach and cook for a minute before adding in the roasted sweet potatoes and Brussel sprouts.

9. Bring another skillet to heat over medium temperatures. Drizzle some oil if necessary and crack in the desired number of eggs. Preferably 1 per person.

10. Prepare the eggs to the desired completion.

11. Serve and enjoy with some parsley garnish.

Quick and Easy Greek Salad

Time: 10 minutes | Servings 1
Kcal 390, Carbs 53.8g/1.89oz, Proteins 19.1g/0.67oz, Fats 11.5g/0.4oz, Fiber 10.8g/0.38oz

Ingredients

- 1 full tomato
- ¼ red onion
- 3 black olives
- ¼ yellow pepper
- 50g/1.76oz salad leaves
- 30g/1.05oz feta cheese
- 1 bagel
- 17g/1 tablespoon fat-free vinaigrette

Preparation

1. Begin by chopping the pepper, onions, olives, and tomatoes.
2. Combine the chopped veggies with the salad leaves and top with the dressing.
3. Now put in the diced Feta cheese.
4. Finally, toast the bagel before serving.

Mediterranean Breakfast Scrambled Eggs

Time: 15 minutes | Servings 2
Kcal 249, Carbs 13.3g/0.47oz, Fats 17g/0.59oz, Proteins 13.5g/0.47oz, Fiber 3.2g/0.11oz

Ingredients

- Freshly chopped parsley for serving
- 15ml/1 tablespoon of oil
- A pinch of black pepper
- 1 diced yellow pepper
- 1g/¼ a teaspoon of dried oregano
- 2 sliced spring onions
- 4 eggs
- 8 quartered cherry tomatoes
- 17g/1 tablespoon of capers
- 34g/2 tablespoons of sliced black olives

Preparation

1. Using a medium frying pan, bring the oil to heat over medium temperatures before adding the spring onions and diced pepper.

2. Allow cooking for 2 minutes till just tender before adding in the capers, tomatoes, and olives and cook for an additional minute.

3. Crack the 4 eggs into the cooked veggies mixture and scramble.

4. Sprinkle in the dried oregano, salt, and black pepper then stir using a spoon continuously till the eggs are well cooked.

5. Serve and enjoy it with some fresh parsley atop for garnish.

Egg Breakfast with Ham

Time: 25 minutes | Servings 6
Kcal 109, Carbs 1.8g/0.06oz, Fats 6.7g/0.23oz, Proteins 9.3g/0.32oz, Fiber 1.8g/0,06oz

Ingredients

- Fresh basil for serving
- 9 slices of thin cut deli ham
- 25ml/1½ tablespoons of pesto sauce
- ½ a cup of canned roasted red pepper
- A pinch of pepper
- 32g/¼ a cup of fresh spinach
- A pinch of salt
- 5 large eggs
- 32g/¼ a cup of crumbled feta cheese

Preparation

1. Bring the oven to a temperature of 204°C/400°F.
2. Generously, coat a muffin dish with cooking spray.
3. For each muffin tin, line with 1½ piece of ham leaving no space for eggs to explode from.
4. Put some roasted red pepper at the bottom of each tin before topping with 1 tablespoon of minced spinach.
5. Finally, layer, the pepper, and spinach with some feta cheese. Do this to every muffin tin.
6. In a good-sized mixing bowl, crack the egg and whisk in some pepper and salt thoroughly.
7. Now divide the mixture among the 6 tins.
8. Allow cooking in the oven till the eggs are set and puffy.
9. Once cooked, remove from the tins, add drizzle with some pesto sauce atop.
10. Garnish with basil and serve.

Avocado Tomato Gouda Socca Pizza

Time: 30 minutes | Servings 2
Kcal 416, Carbs 36.6g/1,29oz, Fats 24.5g/0.86oz, Proteins 15.4g/0.54oz, Fiber 9.6g/0.33oz

Ingredients

For the Crust

- 4g/1 teaspoon of onion powder
- 150g/1¼ a cup of chickpea bean flour
- 4g/1 teaspoon of minced garlic
- 300ml/1¼ cups of cold water
- 30ml/2 tablespoons of olive oil
- A pinch of salt
- A pinch of pepper

For the toppings

- Red pepper flakes
- 1 sliced Roma tomatoes
- A pinch of salt and pepper
- ½ avocado
- Sprouted greens
- 56g/2oz of thinly sliced Gouda
- 34g/2 tablespoons of chopped green onions
- 60ml/¼ a cup of tomato sauce

Preparation

1. Using a medium-sized bowl, combine the flour, seasoning, water, and some olive oil before whisking carefully till smooth. Allow the batter to sit for 20 minutes.

2. Bring your oven to heat up before putting your pan in the oven to preheat as well for approximately 10 minutes.

3. Meanwhile, slice and chop all the veggies.

4. After 10 minutes, remove the pan and put in 1 tablespoon of oil, and swirl to coat evenly.

5. Release the chickpea batter into the pan then tilt to cover and spread evenly.

6. Using a temperature of 218°C/425°F in the oven, put the pan back and allow cooking for 8 minutes or just till the batter begins to set. Remember the time is relative to the size of your pan. If it's bigger than normal, the batter will be thin hence requiring less time to set.

7. Now, spread the sauce atop then put the avocado slices and tomato on top before adding the Gouda slices on top of the avocado and tomato slice.

8. Return the pan to the oven and allow cooking till the socca is brown and crispy on the outside and all the cheese has melted.

9. Once done, the pizza should easily slide off the pan to a heat-safe plate.

10. Top with some sprouts, onions, and some red pepper flakes.

11. Pour a generous amount of olive oil before serving.

Greek Omelet Casserole

Time: 45 minutes | Servings 12 pieces
Kcal 186, Carbs 5g/0.17oz, Fats 13g/0.45oz, Proteins 10g/0.35oz, Fiber 1g/0.035oz

Ingredients

- 60ml/4 tablespoons of divided olive oil
- 12 large eggs
- 4g/1 teaspoon of salt
- 500ml/2 cups of whole milk
- 4g/1 teaspoon of lemon pepper
- 220g/12oz of fresh spinach
- 4g/1 teaspoon of dried oregano
- 2 minced garlic cloves
- 17g/1 tablespoon of fresh chopped dill
- 340g/12oz of artichoke salad
- 140g/5oz of crumbled sundried tomato feta cheese

Preparation

1. Bring the oven to a temperature of 162°C/375°F.
2. Meanwhile, chop the artichoke salad and herbs.
3. Bring the oil to heat on a skillet over medium temperatures then quickly sauté the spinach until just wilted.
4. Spread the spinach and artichokes over the dish.
5. Now, crack the eggs into a mixing bowl and add in the lemon, herbs, pepper, salt, and milk.
6. Empty the contents of the mixing bowl over the baking sheet and top with some crumbled feta cheese.
7. Allow baking in the oven for 40 minutes until set and firm at the center.

Cauliflower Fritters with Hummus

Time: 1 hour 20 minutes | Servings 4
Kcal 333, Carbs 44.7g/1.57oz, Fats 12.6g/0.44oz, Proteins 13.6g/0.48oz, Fiber 12.8g/0.45oz

Ingredients

- Diced green onions
- 2 425g/15oz cans of divided chickpeas
- Hummus of your choice
- 45ml/3 tablespoons of divided olive oil and some more for frying
- A pinch of black pepper
- 120g/1 cup of finely chopped onions
- A pinch of salt
- 4 garlic cloves minced
- 240g/2 cups of cauliflower reduced to small chunks

Preparation

1. Bring the oven to a temperature of 204°C/400°F.

2. Drain and rinse 1 can of the chickpeas then dry them between two paper towels.

3. Move all the dried chickpeas into a mixing bowl and add 1 tablespoon of olive oil and toss well to combine.

4. Using a large frying pan, spread out the chickpeas evenly. Don't overcrowd then add some pepper and salt atop.

5. Cook for 20 minutes then toss and cook for an additional 10 minutes till nice and crispy.

6. Move the baked chickpeas into a food processor. Blitz till they are small and crumbly. Ensure they don't turn into flour. Put it into a smaller bowl and put away.

7. Heat the remainder of the oil in a large skillet preferably over medium temperature.

8. Throw in the garlic and onions, cook till they turn golden brown before putting in the cauliflower, and cook for another 2 minutes till all turns golden.

9. Reduce the heat and cover. Allow the cauliflower to cook for another 5 minutes until it gets fork tender.

10. Once cooked, move the contents of the pan into a food processor.

11. Rinse and drain the remaining can of chickpeas and toss into the food processor as well with some pepper and salt.

12. Continuously, blend till the mixture forms a ball. Only stop to scrape the sides and the bottom of the blender.

13. Move all the mixture in the blender to a mixing bowl. Sprinkle atop some of the chickpea crumbles and toss to mix well.

14. Heat a little oil on the pan over medium temperatures.

15. Now, working in batches cook the chickpea and cauliflower patties for 3 minutes flipping and cooking again till both sides are done.

16. Serve with some green onions and hummus atop.

The Greek Sushi Salad

Time: 20 minutes | Servings 12 rolls
Kcal 54, Carbs 5.2g/0.18oz, Fats 2.2g/0.07oz, Proteins 4g/0.14oz, Fiber 0.6g/0.02oz

Ingredients

- 30g/¼ a cup of crumbled feta cheese
- 1 cucumber
- 30g/¼ a cup of finely diced red onions
- 120g/½ a cup of plain Greek yogurt
- ½ finely chopped bell pepper
- 1 minced garlic clove
- A pinch of pepper and salt
- 4g/1 teaspoon of fresh dill

Preparation

1. Begin by chopping the extreme ends of the cucumber off.
2. Using a vegetable peeler or mandolin, thinly peel the cucumber along the length.
3. Dry the pieces in between paper towels and put away for now.
4. Next, make the Tzatziki by mixing the lemon, dill, yogurt, garlic, salt, and pepper.
5. Spread the freshly made Tzatziki on the slices of the cucumber.
6. Add on top some feta, pepper, and onion.
7. Roll then secure using a toothpick.
8. Do the same till you exhaust all the ingredients.

Banana Split Yogurt

Time: 5 minutes | Servings 2
Kcal 281, Carbs 2g/0.07oz, Fats 29g/1oz, Protein 4g/0.14oz, Fiber 4g/0.14oz

Ingredients

- 250ml/1 cup of Greek yogurt
- ½ sliced banana
- 10ml/2 teaspoons of jam
- 8g/2 teaspoons of cacao nibs

Preparation

1. Combine all the ingredients in a single bowl and serve!

Mediterranean Lunch Recipes

The Israeli Pasta Salad

Time: 15 minutes | Servings 8
Kcal 401, Carbs 64g/2.25oz, Fats 10g/0.3oz, Proteins 15g/0.53oz, Fiber 12g/0.42oz

Ingredients

- Fresh crack black pepper
- 220g/½ lb small bow tie pasta
- A pinch of salt
- 40g/⅓ a cup of finely diced cucumber
- 4g/1 teaspoon of dried oregano
- 40g/⅓ a cup of finely diced radishes
- A bunch of fresh thyme leaves
- 40g/⅓ a cup of finely diced tomatoes
- 40g/⅓ a cup of finely diced feta cheese
- 40g/⅓ a cup of finely diced yellow bell peppers
- 40g/⅓ a cup of diced pepperoncini
- 40g/⅓ a cup of orange bell pepper
- 40g/⅓ a cup of finely diced red onions
- 40g/⅓ a cup of diced black olives
- 40g/⅓ a cup of halved green olives
- Juice of 1 lemon
- 60ml/¼ cup of olive oil

Preparation

1. In saltwater, cook the pasta just until done, be careful not to overcook. Once done, drain any excess water and rinse in cold water.

2. Now, transfer the drained pasta into a medium bowl and add a generous amount of olive oil for them not to stick to one another.

3. Combine with the thyme, oregano, and veggies. Sprinkle atop with some pepper and salt.

4. Put in ¼ a cup of olive oil and the juice from 1 lemon before mixing well.

5. Now, mix the feta cheese in.

6. Put in the refrigerator overnight before serving.

7. Taste and adjust the seasoning accordingly.

8. Enjoy your salad with some thyme garnish.

Cauliflower Pizza and Grilled Vegetables with Greek-Style Yogurt Pesto

Time: 1 hour 20 minutes | Servings 4
Kcal 331, Carbs 23.7g/0.83oz, Fats 16.3g/0.57oz, Proteins 27g/0.95oz, Fiber 7.7g/0.27oz

Ingredients

- Fresh basil
- 12 cups of cauliflower florets
- 60g/½ a cup of grated parmesan
- 30g/1½ tablespoons of minced garlic
- 30ml/2 tablespoons of olive oil
- 2g/½ a teaspoon of salt
- Sliced Roma tomatoes
- 4g/1 teaspoon of Italian seasoning
- 1 small sliced zucchini
- A pinch of pepper
- 100g/3.5oz of divided and grated parmesan cheese
- 34ml/2 tablespoons of minced garlic
- 2 large egg whites
- 60g/½ a cup of coarsely cut fresh basil
- 125ml/½ a cup of plain Greek yogurt

Preparation

1. Bring the oven to a temperature of 204°C/400°F then line a pizza pan with parchment paper.

2. Working in batches, put the cauliflower florets and blitz to rice-like size.

3. Once done, transfer the cauliflower into a microwaveable bowl.

4. Microwave for 15 minutes stirring halfway through and set it aside to cool.

5. Once cool, transfer the cauliflower rice into paper towels to dry the excess moisture. This will go a long way in making a perfect crust.

6. Now move all the dry cauliflower rice into a large bowl and add in the Italian sauce, garlic, some salt, 1⅓ cups of parmesan, and a pinch of pepper.

7. Combine up everything before adding in the egg whites and stir some more.

8. Divide the seasoned cauliflower into 4 balls and spread on the pizza pan leaving an inch for the crust.

9. Cook in the oven for 30 minutes till golden brown.

10. Meanwhile, put garlic, basil, and the Greek yogurt and process till even and smooth.

11. Gently add some olive oil to the mixture while the processor is on then put it aside.

12. Bring your grill to a medium to high temperature.

13. In a medium mixing bowl, combine the tomatoes, zucchini, and olive oil before topping with some pepper and salt.

14. Put the zucchini mixture in the grill and cook for 3 minutes till charred.

15. Once the pizza is done, remove from the oven, top with the remainder of the cheese atop.

16. Cook in the oven till all the cheese has melted.

17. On each pizza, spread the sauce well before topping with grilled veggies and finish off with the last batch of the remaining cheese.

18. Grill till all the cheese melts.

19. Enjoy while hot.

Greek Farro Salad

Time: 1 hour | Servings 6
Kcal 365, Carbs 43g/1.5oz, Fats 17g/0.59oz, Proteins 13g/0.45oz, Fiber 9g/0.31oz

Ingredients

Salad

- 1 425g/15oz can of drained and rinsed chickpeas
- 15ml/1 tablespoon of olive oil
- 40g/¾ a cup of crumbled feta cheese
- 200g/1½ cups of pearled farro
- A pint of halved cherry tomatoes
- 300ml/1¼ cups of water
- 1 small chopped green bell pepper
- 550ml/2½ cups of low sodium vegetable broth
- 1 medium peeled and chopped cucumber
- 250g/2 cups of chopped baby spinach leaves
- ½ thinly sliced red onion

Dressing

- 60ml/¼ a cup of olive oil
- 30ml/2 tablespoons of freshly squeezed lemon juice.
- A pinch of red pepper flakes
- 15ml/1 tablespoon of red wine vinegar
- 1g/¼ a teaspoon of salt
- 15ml/1 tablespoon of honey
- 1g/¼ a teaspoon oregano

Preparation

Preparing the Salad

1. Put a medium skillet on medium heat then add in the olive oil. Put in the farro then proceed to cook for a minute stirring severally.

2. Now pour in the broth and water then bring to boil under high heat.

3. Once the liquid boils, reduce the temperatures to medium and allow everything to simmer for approximately 30 minutes till the farro tenders up.

4. Now, remove any excess liquid before moving to a bowl.

5. While hot, toss in the baby spinach then allow everything to cool.

6. Put in the cucumber, tomato, chickpeas, feta, onions, and pepper then combine.

Preparing the dressing

1. Combine every ingredient for making the dressing in a large mixing bowl and stir thoroughly.

2. Release some of the dressing into the bowl with the farro. Mix well before tasting. Add in the rest to your desired taste.

3. Adjust the seasoning if necessary before serving immediately.

One-Pot Greek Chicken and Lemon Rice

Time: 1 hour | Servings 5
Kcal 667, Carbs 34.2g/1.2oz, Fats 23.4g/0.82oz, Proteins 75.9g/2.67oz, Fiber 1.9g/0.06oz

Ingredients

For the marinade and chicken

- A pinch of salt
- 5 chicken thighs with bone-in and skin on
- 4 minced garlic cloves

- 2 lemons. 60ml/4 tablespoons of lemon juice + the zest
- 17g/1 tablespoon of dried oregano

For the rice

- A pinch of black pepper
- 25ml/1½ tablespoons of separated olive oil
- 3g/¾ a teaspoon of salt
- 1 finely diced onion
- 17ml/1 tablespoon of dried oregano
- 180g/1 cup of uncooked long-grain rice
- 185ml/¾ a cup of water
- 375ml/1½ cups of chicken broth
- Fresh lemon zest for garnish

Preparation

1. In a sealable plastic bag, combine all the chicken and marinade ingredients, combine and refrigerate overnight, or a minimum of 20 minutes.

2. Bring the oven to a temperature of 180°C/350°F.

3. Remove the chicken and set the marinade aside.

4. Bring ½ a tablespoon of olive oil to heat in a heavy-base and deep skillet.

5. Cook the chicken having the skin side down until nice and brown before flipping to the other side and cook till brown as well.

6. Drain any excess fat from the pan with a paper towel before returning to the stove.

7. Heat 1 tablespoon of olive oil under medium to high temperatures before putting in the onions and cook till translucent.

8. Put in the remaining rice ingredients before topping with the marinade.

9. Let everything simmer for roughly 30 seconds before putting in the chicken and covering the skillet.

10. Transfer to the oven and allow cooking for 35 minutes with the lid on and an additional 10 minutes till the rice gets tender and all the liquid is absorbed.

11. Once done, take out of the oven and allow cooking for 10 minutes before serving with fresh parsley for garnish.

The Mediterranean Vegan Salad

Time: 15 minutes | Servings 4

Kcal 195, Carbs 10.9g/0.38oz, Proteins 2g/0.07oz, Fats 17.1g/0.6oz, Fiber 5.5g/0.19oz

Ingredients

- 3 large tomatoes
- Pepper and salt
- 32g/¼ a cup of baby tomatoes
- Juice from ½ a lemon
- 1 avocado
- 30ml/2 tablespoons of balsamic vinegar
- 1 Persian cucumber
- 30ml/2 tablespoons olive oil
- ½ red onion
- 2g/½ a teaspoon of Dijon mustard
- Fresh basil

Preparation

1. Roughly cut the cucumber, onions, avocados, and tomatoes then put them on a serving dish.

2. Slice the baby tomatoes into halves and add to the dish.

3. Sprinkle chopped basil over the salad.

4. In a separate bowl, combine and whisk balsamic vinegar, olive oil, mustard, lemon juice pepper, and salt.

5. Empty the dressing atop the salad and serve.

Greek-Style Meatball with Tzatziki

Time: 26 minutes | Servings 4
Kcal 429, Carbs 38g/1.34oz, Fats 19g/0.67oz, Proteins 28g/0.98oz, Fiber 3g/0.11oz

Ingredients

Meatball

- 30ml/2 tablespoons of olive oil
- 450g/1 lb ground turkey
- Pepper and salt
- 30g/¼ a cup of finely diced red onion
- 130g/1 cup of fresh chopped spinach
- 2 minced garlic cloves
- 17g/1 tablespoon of oregano

Tzatziki

- 4 whole wheat flatbread
- 250ml/½ a cup of Greek yogurt
- 1 cup of diced cucumber
- 30ml/2 tablespoons of lemon juice
- 120g/1 cup of diced tomato
- 2g/½ a teaspoon of dried dill
- ½ a cup of thinly sliced red onions
- 2g/½ a teaspoon of garlic powder
- Salt

Preparation

1. Using a large bowl, combine the red onions, garlic, spinach, salt, pepper, and ground turkey. Mix using your fingers thoroughly until you achieve a single piece of meatball.

2. Divide the meatball into 12 equal but smaller meatballs.

3. Bring a large skillet to heat under medium to high temperatures. Once hot enough, pour some olive oil before putting in the meatballs.

4. Working in batches cook each meatball till browned all over then set aside for some time.

5. Meanwhile, add the lemon juice, grated cucumber, yogurt, garlic powder, salt, and dill to a smaller mixing bowl and stir.

6. Warm the flatbread slightly before adding 3 meatballs cucumber, tomato, sliced onions, and top off with the Tzatziki sauce.

7. Enjoy!

Greek Salad Tacos

Time: 30 minutes | Servings 4
Kcal 54, Carbs 5.2g/0.18oz, Protein 4g/0.142oz, Fat 1.5g/0.05oz, Fiber 0.6g/0.02oz

Ingredients

- 8 flour tortillas
- 250g/2 cups of grilled chicken
- 125ml/½ a cup of any Greek dressing of your choice
- 1 cup Dannon Oikos Dips cucumber and dill
- 480g/4 cups of shredded romaine lettuce
- 60g/½ a cup of sliced black olives
- 120g/1 cup of diced tomato
- 120g/1 cup of crumbled feta cheese
- 90g/¾ a cup of diced cucumber
- 30g/¼ a cup of diced cilantro

Preparation

1. In a mixing bowl, combine all ingredients leaving out the tacos, feta, and the cucumber and dill dressing, then mix well.

2. Heat your tortillas on both sides to make them pliable.

3. Now fill each tortilla with the salad before topping with the crumbled feta and the dressing to make the taco.

4. Enjoy!

Greek Quesadillas

Time: 30 minutes | Servings 8
Kcal 384, Carbs 32.6g/1.14oz, Fats 18.5g/0.65oz, Proteins 14.4g/0.5oz, Fiber 3g/0.1oz

Ingredients

- 17g/1 tablespoon of fresh dill
- 8 flour tortilla
- 120g/1 cup of crumbled feta cheese
- 1 280g/10oz package of frozen and chopped spinach (drained and thawed)
- 120g/1 cup of shredded mozzarella
- 60g/½ a cup julienned sun-dried tomatoes in olive oil, drained
- 60g/½ a cup of chopped and pitted kalamata olives

For the Tzatziki

- 30ml/2 tablespoons of olive oil
- 250ml/1 cup of plain Greek yogurt
- Ground black pepper and Kosher salt
- 1 diced English cucumber
- 4g/1 teaspoon of freshly chopped mint
- 2 pressed cloves of garlic
- 4g/1 teaspoon of lemon zest
- 17g/1 tablespoon of freshly chopped dill
- 15ml/1 tablespoon of freshly squeezed lemon juice.

Preparation

1. Begin by making the Tzatziki sauce, combine the cucumber, garlic, lemon juice, dill, lemon zest, yogurt, and mint in a small mixing bowl then sprinkle over with some pepper and salt.

2. Top with some olive oil and mix well before putting in the refrigerator for 10 minutes.

3. Bring the oven to a temperature of 204°C/400°F before lining the baking tray with parchment paper.

4. Having one tortillas piece at the bottom arrange to have the spinach first, sundried tomatoes, olives, and lastly the cheese before topping with a final layer of tortilla. Repeat till you make 4 quesadillas.

5. Cook the quesadillas in the oven till the cheese has melted.

6. Serve with the Tzatziki sauce on the side and dill garnish atop.

Mediterranean Herb Shrimp with Penne

Time: 30 minutes | Serving 6
Kcal 291, Carbs 36g/1.26oz, Fats 5g/0.17oz, Proteins 24g/0.84oz, Fiber 2g/0.07oz

Ingredients

- Grated parmesan cheese
- 220g/8oz penne pasta
- 2g/½ a teaspoon of sea salt
- 450g/1 lb deveined and peeled shrimp
- 8g/2 teaspoons of herb seasoning
- 240g/2 cups of broccoli florets
- 100g/4oz of cubed Neufchatel cheese
- 250ml/1 cup of fat-free half and half

Preparation

1. Cook the pasta according to the directions in the package adding in the broccoli and shrimp in the last 3 minutes. Drain any excess water once cooked.

2. In a small saucepan, simmer the half and half. Reduce the heat to low before adding in the salt, cream cheese, and seasoning. Combine until the cheese melts and the sauce is smooth and blended.

3. In a serving bowl, put the shrimp, broccoli, and pasta then top with the sauce.

4. Serve immediately and enjoy!

Mediterranean Salad with Balsamic Chicken

Time: 30 minutes | Servings 6
Kcal 495, Carbs 52g/1.83oz, Fats 5g/0.17oz, Proteins 32g/1.13oz, Fiber 2g/0.07oz

Ingredients

- Fresh ground pepper and salt
- 340g/¾ lb of 18 chunks of skinless chicken breasts
- 120g/1 cup of rinsed, drained, and cooked chickpeas
- 18 cherry tomatoes
- 240g/2 cups of torn fresh basil
- 1 medium zucchini cut into 18 rounds
- 10 cups of baby arugula leaves
- 1 large yellow-red pepper sliced into 18 pieces.
- 200g/7oz round whole wheat bread loaf sliced into 4 pieces
- 1 small sweet onion sliced into 18 pieces
- 60ml/4 tablespoons of extra virgin olive oil
- 45ml/3 tablespoons of balsamic vinegar
- 15ml/1 tablespoon of dijon mustard

Preparation

1. Assemble 6 skewers. Into each skewer, thread a piece of chicken, a tomato, zucchini, pepper, and an onion. Repeat the order three times till each skewer holds 3 pieces of each of the aforementioned ingredients.

2. Do the same to the remainder of the skewers.

3. Apply some vinaigrette to each skewer, before oiling the grill grates and preheating the grill to preferably a medium.

4. Cook the skewers over the grill turning frequently till the veggies are tender and the chicken is nice and cooked through.

5. Now, grill the bread pieces on both sides till they get brown.

6. To serve, arrange equal amounts of basil, arugula, and chickpeas on 4 plates.

7. On each plate, add 1½ of the baked skewer contents and finish off with a drizzle of vinaigrette.

Mediterranean Dinner Recipes

Mediterranean Stuffed Sweet Potatoes with Chickpeas and Avocado Tahini

Time: 50 minutes | Servings 8
Kcal 308, Carbs 38g/1.34oz, Fats 2g/0.07oz, Proteins 7g/0.24oz, Fiber 8g/0.28oz

Ingredients

For the chickpeas

- 8 medium-sized rinsed sweet potatoes
- 1g/¼ a teaspoon of salt
- 425/15oz drained and rinsed chickpeas
- 17g/1 tablespoon of fresh oregano
- ½ diced red bell pepper
- 17g/1 tablespoon of freshly chopped parsley
- 50ml/3 tablespoons of extra virgin olive oil
- 1 crushed garlic clove
- 15ml/1 tablespoon of fresh lemon juice
- 15ml/1 tablespoon of lemon zest

For the avocado Tahini sauce

- 15ml/1 tablespoon of fresh lemon juice
- 1 medium ripe avocado
- 17g/1 tablespoon of fresh parsley
- 60ml/¼ a cup of tahini
- 1 crushed clove of garlic
- 60ml/¼ a cup of water.

For the toppings

- Crumbled up feta
- 30g/¼ a cup of pepitas, hulled pumpkin seeds

Preparation

1. Bring the oven to a temperature of 204°C/400°F.

2. Make some holes in the sweet potatoes using a knife or a fork to let out the air.

3. Now cook in the oven for 45 minutes until they get tender. You will know they are ready when they are nice and tender when touched. The cooking time is relative to the sizes of your sweet potatoes. The larger they are the more time they will take.

4. Meanwhile, combine all chickpeas and all the ingredients in a medium cooking bowl.

5. Toss well so that the chickpeas combine well with the marinade. Put aside for a while.

6. For the tahini sauce, combine all ingredients and put in a blender.

7. Blend till you achieve a uniform consistency. If the sauce is too thick for your liking add in 2 tablespoons of water and blend again.

8. Once done, move the sauce to a separate small bowl and put it aside.

9. Now we combine everything. Remove the sweet potatoes from the oven and allow cooling for a few minutes.

10. Make slits through each avocado and add a spoonful of the marinated chickpeas inside.

11. Add the tahini sauce atop before adding the pepitas and feta cheese on top.

12. Enjoy them fresh or store in the fridge not more than 2 days.

The Greek Goddess Bowl

Time: 30 minutes | Servings 2
Kcal 519, Carbs 49.8g/1.75oz, Fats 34.5g/1.21oz, Proteins 12g/0.42oz, Fiber 13.3g/0.46oz

Ingredients

For the chickpeas

- A pinch of salt
- 425g/15oz of rinsed and drained chickpeas
- 15ml/1 tablespoon of maple syrup
- 15ml/1 tablespoon of avocado oil
- 17g/1 tablespoon of the shawarma spice blend

For the bowl

- 1 thinly sliced carrot
- 180ml/¾ a cup of vegan Tzatziki
- 1 thinly sliced cucumber
- 1 batch of coarsely chopped parsley
- 60g/½ a cup of chopped green olives
- 60g/½ a cup of halved cherry tomatoes

Preparation

1. Bring the oven to a temperature of 190°C/375°F then make ready your baking sheet.

2. In a mixing bowl, combine the chickpeas, shawarma, oil, maple syrup, and some salt then combine carefully.

3. Transfer the seasoned chickpeas to the baking sheet before putting in the oven. Cook for 25 minutes till crispy.

4. To prepare the bowl, combine the parsley, tomatoes, olives, carrots, and cucumber then divide it into two serving bowl.

5. Now put the baked chickpeas atop and drizzle with some freshly squeezed lemon juice if desired.

6. Enjoy with a dipping sauce of your liking.

Greek Zucchini and Walnut Salad

Time: 20 minutes | Serves 2
Kcal 595, Carbs 8g/0.28oz, Fats 58g/2.05oz, Protein 9g/0.32oz, Fiber 7g/0.24oz

Ingredients

- 32g/¼ a cup of freshly cut chives
- 15ml/1 tablespoon of olive oil
- 2 zucchini
- 1 finely minced clove of garlic
- 10ml/2 teaspoons lemon juice
- 190ml/¾ a cup of vegan mayonnaise
- 30ml/2 tablespoons of olive oil
- 2g/½ a teaspoon of salt
- 1g/¼ a teaspoon of chili powder
- A head of romaine lettuce
- 100g/3½ of chopped walnuts
- 115g/4oz of arugula lettuce
- Pepper and salt

Preparation

1. Combine and whisk all the ingredients for making the dressing. Once mixed thoroughly, set aside to develop and blend flavors.
2. Put the romaine lettuce, chives, and arugula in a single bowl.
3. Cut and split the zucchini along the length then remove the seeds. Further cut the zucchini across into half-inch slices.
4. On a pan, bring olive oil to heat before adding the chopped zucchini. Add some pepper and a pinch of salt to your liking.
5. Sauté till you achieve a light brown color.
6. Combine the salad and zucchini before mixing thoroughly.
7. Roast nuts in the same pan. Add some pepper and salt to taste.
8. Serve the nuts on the salad and top with the salad dressing.

Easy Salad with Chicken Skewers (Grilled)

Time: 1 hour | Servings 4
Kcal 365, Carbs 11g/0.38oz, Fats 22g/0.77oz, Proteins 33g/1.16oz, Fiber 3g/0.1oz

Ingredients

- 30ml/2 tablespoons of olive oil
- 3 chicken breasts sliced into ½ an inch chunks
- 30ml/2 tablespoons of plain nonfat yogurt
- Shitake mushrooms
- 5ml/1 teaspoon lemon juice
- 45ml/2 tablespoon lemon juice
- 20ml/4 teaspoons of white wine vinegar
- 30ml/2 tablespoons of lavender balsamic vinegar
- 20ml/4 teaspoons pesto
- 45ml/2 tablespoons of olive oil
- 30g/¼ a cup of feta cheese
- 4g/1 teaspoon of dried basil
- 50g/3 tablespoons of kalamata olives
- 1 minced garlic clove
- 100g/6 tablespoons of sliced roasted red pepper
- 2g/½ a teaspoon of parsley
- 40g/⅓ a cup of chopped artichoke hearts
- 2g/½ a teaspoon of onion powder
- 80g/¾ a cup of sliced tomatoes
- A pinch of Kosher salt
- 80g/¾ a cup of diced cucumber
- A pinch of red pepper
- 30g/¼ a cup of sliced green onions
- 500g/4 cups of chopped romaine lettuce
- 500g/4 cups of baby spinach

Preparation

1. To make the salad, layer each plate having the spinach and romaine lettuce at the bottom of the plate.

2. Add some diced cucumber, tomatoes, artichokes, roasted red peppers, the kalamata leaves, and finally feta cheese.

3. For the dressing, combine the lemon juice and white wine vinegar in a medium jar then toss. Add in some oil and the yogurt then shake some more.

4. Make the chicken marinade by combining the balsamic vinegar, lemon juice, garlic, basil, olive oil, red pepper, onion powder, and salt. Drizzle over the chicken and refrigerate for 30 minutes.

5. If you are using wooden skewers, soak in water beforehand then thread on the chicken. Soaking is not necessary for metallic skewers.

6. Thread on the mushrooms and chicken on the skewers to make a kebab.

7. Cook on the grill rotating the skewers frequently until the chicken is cooked.

8. Serve with the salad at the bottom then drizzle over with the vinaigrette before topping with the chicken kebab.

Mediterranean Salmon Souvlaki Bowls

Time: 25 minutes | Servings 3
Kcal 165, Carbs 14.4g/0.51oz, Protein 9g/0.32oz, Fat 9.2g/0.33oz, Fiber 3.8g/0.13oz

Ingredients

- 90ml/6 tablespoons of lemon juice
- 45ml/3 tablespoons of olive oil
- 450g/1 lb of fresh salmon fish cut into 4 pieces
- 30ml/2 tablespoon
- 30ml/2 spoons of balsamic vinegar

- 17g/1 tablespoon of fresh dill
- 17g/1 tablespoon of fresh oregano
- ½ cloves of garlic minced and grated
- 17g/1 tablespoon of pepper
- 2g/½ a teaspoon of salt
- 4g/1 teaspoon of pepper

For the Bowls

- 2 quartered red peppers
- 128g/1 cup of dry pearl couscous or even farro
- 128g/1 cup of cherry tomatoes halved
- 230g/8oz of feta cheese crumbled
- Juice from one lemon
- 2 sliced Persian cucumbers
- 30ml/2 tablespoons of olive oil
- 64g/½ a cup of Kalamata olives
- 1-inch zucchini cut into ¼ rounds

Preparation

1. In a suitable bowl, combine the lemon juice, vinegar, smoked paprika, oregano, dill, garlic, pepper and salt, and olive oil.

2. Add the salmon and toss very well, making sure the salmon is well coated in the seasonings.

3. Cook the couscous or farro according to the instructions and in another separate bowl, combine the zucchini, olive oil, salt, red peppers, and all and also toss well to coat the veggies.

4. Heat the grill to medium heat and then transfer the salmon to the grill already preheated for some minutes until the salmon is done.

5. Remove it and add the zucchini and bell peppers, grill for some minutes per side until the marks appear, and then remove everything from the grill.

6. Assemble the farro or the couscous accordingly, add the veggies, and drizzle with olive oil.

7. Top everything with the tzatziki sauce and garnish with some fresh herbs.

Roasted Herb Salmon

Time: 45 minutes | Servings 4

Kcal 322, Carbs 6g/0.21oz, Fats 20g/0.7oz, Proteins 30g/1.05oz, Fiber 2g/0.07oz

Ingredients

- 2 tomatoes thinly sliced
- 110g/4oz of salmon fillets sliced into 1½ inches thick
- 1 thinly sliced yellow onions
- 30ml/2 tablespoons Dijon mustard
- Cooking spray
- 30ml/2 tablespoon lemon juice
- 2g/½ a teaspoon of ground black pepper
- 17g/1 tablespoon of minced fresh thyme
- A pinch of salt
- 17g/1 tablespoon of minced fresh rosemary
- 4g/1 teaspoon of dried oregano.

Preparation

1. Begin by making 2-inch long slits at the top of each fillet.
2. In a shallow mixing bowl, combine rosemary, thyme, lemon, mustard, pepper, salt, and oregano then mix thoroughly.
3. Put in the salmon making sure they are well coated on the two sides.
4. Put into a sealable plastic bag then put it in the refrigerator for 20 minutes.
5. Now, bring the oven to a temperature of 450°F.
6. Spray a baking sheet with a thin layer of cooking spray before putting at the bottom onions and tomato slice.
7. Top with the marinated salmon then pour atop with the marinade.
8. Cook for 15 minutes till the salmon is nice and tender.

Pasta and Basil Tapenade

Time: 30 minutes | Servings 5
Kcal 375, Carbs 59g/2.08oz, Fats 10g/0.35oz, Proteins 11g/0.38oz, Fiber 4g/0.14oz

Ingredients

- Freshly grated parmesan cheese
- A pinch of salt
- 45ml/3 tablespoons of extra virgin olive oil
- 250ml/½ a cup of water
- 450g/1 lb linguine
- 120g/1 cup of packed fresh basil leaves
- 15ml/1 tablespoon of fresh lemon juice
- 120g/1 cup of pitted kalamata olives
- 2 medium cloves of garlic

Preparation

1. In a large pot, bring some salted water to boil.
2. Now wash the basil and parsley leaves in running water then dry before putting them into a food processor.
3. Blitz till pulverized then add in the lemon juice, garlic, and olives and blitz to a smooth puree then move to a large bowl.
4. Put the pasta in the boiling salt water till nice and al dente then drain any excess water and pour in the bowl with the puree.
5. Pour in olive oil immediately and top with some cheese.
6. Combine using tongs to mix up everything.
7. Serve and enjoy!

Mediterranean Flatbread Pizza

Time: 20 minutes | Servings 3
Kcal 450, Carbs 57g/2.01oz, Fats 19g/0.67oz, Proteins 17g/0.59oz, Fiber 9g/0.31oz

Ingredients

- 56g/2oz of crumbled feta cheese with Mediterranean herbs
- 3 pieces of pita bread
- ¼ small red onion
- 40g/⅔ a cup of drained and rinsed cannellini beans
- ½ a medium avocado
- 200g/2 cups of packed baby spinach
- 60g/½ a cup of marinated artichoke hearts
- 15ml/1 tablespoon of extra virgin olive oil
- 60g/½ a cup of cherry tomatoes
- 30g/¼ a cup of natural almonds
- A pinch of pepper
- 30g/¼ a cup of torn basil leaves
- A pinch of fine sea salt
- 30ml/2 tablespoons of water

Preparation

1. Bring the oven to a temperature of 176°C/350°F.

2. Now put the pita bread on top of the baking sheet.

3. For the white beans and spinach pesto; put the baby spinach, white beans, olive oil, water, basil, almonds, pepper, and sea salt in the food processor. Pulse continuously till smooth.

4. Apply the pesto to the pita bread using a spoon.

5. Chop the onions and avocado into small pieces, halve the tomatoes, and chop the artichokes before arranging on the pizza.

6. Top each pizza with crumbled feta cheese then finish off with salt atop.

7. Cook in the oven until the bread gets slightly crispy.

8. Once done, allow cooling for a few minutes before slicing the flatbreads into two.

The Mediterranean Chopped Salad

Time: 20 minutes | Servings 2
Kcal 190, Carbs 14g/0.49oz, Proteins 14g/0.49oz, Fats 8g/0.28oz, Fiber 3g/0.11oz

Ingredients

Lemon Vinaigrette

- Himalayan pink salt
- 60ml/¼ a cup of Meyer lemon juice
- 60ml/¼ a cup plus extra olive oil

Salad

- 4g/1 teaspoon of chopped basil
- 60g/½ a cup of chopped Persian cucumber
- ½ chopped avocado
- 60g/½ a cup of chopped artichokes
- 17g/1 tablespoon of capers
- 60g/½ a cup of chopped hearts of palm
- 34g/2 tablespoons of chopped red onions
- 60g/½ a cup of chopped tomatoes
- 34g/2 tablespoons of chopped kalamata olives

Preparation

1. For the Vinaigrette, add all the ingredients to a blender and blend till emulsified before adding some salt.
2. Combine the artichoke hearts, hearts of palm, onions, olive, tomatoes, basil, avocadoes, capers, and cucumbers in a salad bowl.
3. Pour the vinaigrette over the salad and mix.
4. Serve and enjoy.

Roasted Vegetable Mediterranean-Style

Time: 45 minutes | Servings 1
Kcal 854, Carbs 20.8g/0.73oz, Proteins 5.4g/0.19oz, Fats 87.1g/3.07oz, Fiber 5.2g/0.17oz

Ingredients

- 🍽 250ml/1 cup of kale cut into ribbons
- 🍽 A pinch of crushed red pepper flakes
- 🍽 60ml/¼ a cup of marinated artichoke hearts
- 🍽 Freshly ground black pepper and sea salt
- 🍽 60ml/¼ a cup of Kalamata olives
- 🍽 17g/1 tablespoon of fresh parsley
- 🍽 32g/¼ a cup of chopped walnuts
- 🍽 17g/1 tablespoon of nutritional yeast
- 🍽 34g/2 tablespoons of chopped sun-dried tomatoes
- 🍽 15ml/1 tablespoon of olive oil
- 🍽 15ml/1 tablespoon of fresh lemon juice
- 🍽 ½ spaghetti squash with seeds removed

Preparation

1. Bring the oven to a temperature of 200°C/400°F before lining the baking sheet with parchment paper.

2. On one half of the baking sheet, place the squashes then top with some olive oil, pepper, and some sea salt.

3. Cook in the oven for 45 minutes having the cut side down.

4. Using a fork, scrape the stands far from the shell before adding some more salt to taste.

5. Now place the artichokes, tomatoes, walnuts, Kalamata olives, and kale atop the squashes.

6. Finally, drizzle with the lemon juice, some olive oil, and top with the freshly chopped parsley.

7. Add some red pepper if you so wish and enjoy it!

28-DAY MEDITERRANEAN DIET MEAL PLAN

Since we acknowledge that the Mediterranean is quite flexible and there is no silver bullet when it comes to this diet. Here is the 28-day meal planner that will enable you to reap maximum benefit out of this diet plan. Here are some of the easy to prepare meals for breakfast, lunch, and dinner.

Day 1

Breakfast: The Mediterranean Breakfast Sandwiches

Time: 25 minutes | Servings 4

Kcal 242, Carbs 25g/0.88oz, Fats 11.7g/0.41oz, Proteins 13g/0.45oz, Fiber 6.2g/0.21oz

Ingredients

- A pinch of finely ground paper
- 4 multigrain sandwich film
- A pinch of kosher salt
- 20ml/4 teaspoons of olive oil
- 70g/4 tablespoons of reduced-fat feta cheese
- 2g/½ a teaspoon of dried and crushed rosemary
- 1 medium tomato sliced into 8 pieces
- 4 large eggs
- 250g/2 cups of baby spinach

Preparation

1. Bring the oven to a temperature of 180°C/350°F.

2. Split the sandwiches before oiling each cut side with olive oil.

3. Cook the sandwich slices in the oven for 5 minutes till the edges start getting brown.

4. In a medium skillet, bring 2teaspoons of olive oil to heat then go ahead and put in the rosemary.

5. Crack the eggs in the oil and rosemary mixture cooking one at a time until just set but the yolk remains runny.

6. Now, on four serving plates, put a sandwich thin at the bottom then top with equal portions of spinach per plate. Put tomato slices over the spinach, the cooked egg, and a tablespoon of feta cheese.

7. Season with some salt before finally topping with a final slice of sandwich.

Lunch: The Israeli Pasta Salad (See page 36)

Dinner: Mediterranean Stuffed Sweet Potatoes with Chickpeas and Avocado Tahini (See page 55)

Day 2

Breakfast: The Mediterranean Easy ShakShuka (See page 20)

Lunch: Baked Salmon with Dill

Time: 15 minutes | Servings 4

Kcal 251, Carbs 1g/0.035oz, Fats 13g/0.45oz, Proteins 34g/1.11oz, Fiber 0g

Ingredients

- 4 lemon wedges
- 4 × 170g/6oz salmon fillets
- A pinch of freshly ground pepper
- 25g/1½ tablespoons of finely chopped fresh dill
- 2g/½ a teaspoon of kosher salt

Preparation

1. Bring the oven to a temperature of 180°C/350°F.
2. Prepare a baking sheet by lightly coating with cooking spray before arranging the fillets.
3. Add some pepper, dill, and salt to taste.
4. Allow cooking in the oven until the fish gets tender to the fork which should take roughly 10 minutes.
5. Serve on 4 plates with lemon wedges on the side.

Dinner: The Greek Goddess Bowl (See page 57)

Day 3

Breakfast: Breakfast Hash with Sweet Potatoes and Brussel Sprouts (See page 22)

Lunch: Cauliflower Pizza and Grilled Vegetables with Greek-Style Yogurt Pesto (See page 38)

Dinner: Mediterranean Barley with Chickpeas
Time: | Servings 4
Kcal 359, Carbs 61g/2.15oz, Fats 5g/0.17oz, Proteins 11g/0.38oz, Fiber 14g/0.49oz

Ingredients

- 34g/2 tablespoons of chopped pistachios
- 120g/1 cup of cooked pearl barley
- 2g/½ a teaspoon of crushed pepper
- 120g/1 cup of packed arugula leaves
- 4g/1 teaspoon of salt
- 120g/1 cup of finely chopped red bell pepper
- 30g/2 tablespoons of extra virgin olive oil
- 50g/3 tablespoons of finely chopped sun-dried tomatoes
- 30ml/2 tablespoons of lemon juice
- 1 440g/15½oz of drained and rinsed unsalted chickpeas

Preparation

1. Prepare and cook the barley according to the directions in the package but do not add any salt during the process.

2. In a large mixing bowl, put the arugula tomatoes, bell pepper, chickpeas, and barley.

3. In a separate smaller mixing bowl, combine the pepper, salt, oil, and lemon juice then whisk thoroughly.

4. Spread over the barley mixture before mixing.

5. Top with some pistachios before serving.

Day 4

Breakfast: The Caprese Avocado Toast

Time: 5 minutes | Servings 2

Kcal 338, Carbs 25.8g/0.91oz, Proteins 12.8g/0.45oz, Fats 20.4g/0.72oz, Fiber 9.2g/0.32oz

Ingredients

- 1 medium avocado, well halved and its pit removed
- 2 slices of a hearty sandwich bread such as the whole wheat bread, sourdough, etc.
- 8 grape tomatoes, halved
- 4 large fresh and good quality ciliegine, or bite-sized mozzarella balls, about 12 of them
- 34g/2 tablespoons of balsamic glaze

Preparation

1. Toast the bread and while it is toasting, proceed to mash all the avocados in a small bowl.

2. Spread the mashed avocado over all the toast and then top each of the slices you have with basil leaves, tomatoes, mozzarella, and finally drizzle on top with balsamic glaze.

3. Serve immediately.

Lunch: One-Pot Greek Chicken and Lemon Rice (See page 43)

Dinner: Greek Zucchini and Walnut Salad (See page 59)

Day 5

Breakfast: Quick and Easy Greek Salad (See page 24)

Lunch: Whole Wheat Couscous with Parmesan and Peas

Time: 20 minutes | Servings 6

Kcal 213, Carbs 36g/1.26oz, Fats 4.2g/0.14oz, Proteins 9.9g/0.34oz, Fiber 6.6g/0.23oz

Ingredients

- 🍽 60g/½ a cup of freshly grated parmesan cheese
- 🍽 1 400g/14.1oz can of low sodium chicken broth
- 🍽 A pinch of freshly ground pepper and salt
- 🍽 60ml/¼ a cup of water
- 🍽 4g/1 teaspoon of freshly grated lemon zest
- 🍽 10ml/2 teaspoons of extra virgin olive oil
- 🍽 34g/2 tablespoons of freshly chopped dill
- 🍽 120g/1 cup of whole wheat couscous
- 🍽 180g/1½ cups of frozen peas

Preparation

1. In a large saucepan, combine water, chicken broth, and olive oil then bring to boil on a stove.
2. Now, pot in the couscous and stir well before covering and allowing it to plump for a while.
3. For the peas, cook per the directions of the package.
4. Finally, add the peas, salt, lemon zest, dill, and pepper to the couscous before mixing.
5. Serve on plates then top with cheese.

Dinner: Easy Salad with Chicken Skewers (Grilled) (See page 60)

Day 6

Breakfast: Mediterranean Breakfast Scrambled Eggs (See page 25)

Lunch: Greek Farro Salad (See page 41)

Dinner: Easy Mediterranean Hummus Chicken Salad Wrap

Time: 5 minutes | Servings 3

Kcal 225, Carbs 20g/0.7oz, Fats 0g, Proteins 21g/0.74oz, Fiber 4g/0.14oz

Ingredients

- 🍽 3 whole wheat tortilla
- 🍽 120g/1 cup of shredded and cooked chicken
- 🍽 60g/½ a cup of hummus

Preparation

1. Using a medium bowl, combine the hummus and the shredded chicken and mix well.

2. Serve equal portions on the tortilla slices and enjoy!

Day 7

Breakfast: Mediterranean Vegan Pancakes

Time: 20 minutes | Serves 2

Kcal 260, Carbs 5.1g/0.18oz., Fats 20.8g/0.73oz., Proteins 9.8g/0.35oz., Fiber 8.8g/0.31oz

Ingredients

- 30ml/2 tablespoons of unsweetened almond butter
- 17g/1 tablespoon of ground flax
- 125g/½ a cup of unsweetened almond milk
- 17g/1 tablespoon of coconut flour
- 2g/½ a teaspoon baking powder
- A pinch of salt if you don't use almond butter
- 30ml/2 tablespoons of olive oil

Preparation

1. Lightly put some olive oil on a pan over low to medium heat.
2. Mix almond butter and almond milk in a bowl.
3. Combine and mix well all the dry ingredients till well blended.
4. Now mix all the wet and dry ingredients until thoroughly blended. Put aside for 5 minutes and let the coconut flour and flux absorb the liquid.
5. Scoop some batter and spread on the pan and cook for 2-5 minutes, flipping the other side when one side is cooked.
6. Top with some almond butter before serving and enjoy!

Lunch: Greek-Style Meatball with Tzatziki (See page 46)

Dinner: Mediterranean Salmon Souvlaki Bowls (See page 62)

Day 8

Breakfast: Egg Breakfast with Ham (See page 36)

Lunch: Greek-Style Turkey Burgers with Yogurt Sauce
Time: 20 minutes | Servings 2

Kcal 204, Carbs 0g, Fats 12g/0.42oz, Proteins 12g/0.42oz, Fiber 4g/0.14oz

Ingredients

For the burgers

- A pinch of ground black pepper
- 450g/1 lb ground turkey
- A pinch of fine-grain salt
- 60g/½ a cup of crumbled feta cheese
- 17g/1 tablespoon of fresh chopped mint
- 15ml/1 tablespoon of milk
- 17g/1 tablespoon of freshly chopped parsley

For the sauce

- A pinch of fine-grain salt
- A container of 170g/6oz of plain Greek yogurt
- 17g/1 tablespoon of fresh chopped mint
- 15ml/1 tablespoon of fresh lemon juice
- 17g/1 tablespoon of freshly chopped parsley
- 1 minced garlic clove

Preparation

1. Using a large mixing bowl, combine the salt, parsley, mint, milk, pepper, and feta cheese.

2. Using your hands, mix the ingredients then make four patties out of the dough.

3. Bring a grill pan or a grill to heat over medium to high temperatures.

4. Now, grill the patties till cooked through.

5. For the yogurt sauce, combine all the ingredients, mix, taste, and adjust the seasoning accordingly.

6. Serve two burgers per serving with the yogurt sauce for dipping.

Dinner: Roasted Herb Salmon (See page 64)

Day 9

Breakfast: Avocado Tomato Gouda Socca Pizza (See page 27)

Lunch: Greek Salad Tacos (See page 48)

Dinner: Vegetarian Stuffed Peppers

Time: 45 minutes | Servings 4

Kcal 389, Carbs 54g/1.9oz, Fats 12g/0.42oz, Proteins 19g/0.67oz, Fiber 23g/0.8oz

Ingredients

- A pinch of salt and black pepper
- 120g/1 cup of uncooked red lentils
- 8g/2 teaspoons of ground cumin
- 60g/½ a cup of rinsed and drained chickpeas
- 30ml/2 tablespoons of olive oil
- 60g/½ a cup of rinsed and drained canned kidney beans
- 2 cloves of minced garlic
- 4 medium bell peppers of any color
- 1 lime juice
- 80g/⅔ a cup of heirloom tomatoes
- ½ diced small avocado
- 60g/½ a cup of red onions slices
- 40g/⅓ cup of chopped parsley
- ½ diced jalapeno
- 40g/⅓ a cup of chopped cilantro

Preparation

1. Cut off the top of the bell peppers and remove the seeds and white pulp from the center.
2. Go ahead and cook the red lentils per the directions in the package.
3. Use a large mixing bowl to collect together the seasoning, beans, and the chopped veggies. Mix well then adjust the seasoning accordingly.
4. Scoop the beans mixture using a spoon into the raw pre-prepared bell peppers.
5. Top with equal amounts of avocado.

Day 10

Breakfast: Vegan Tofu Scramble

Time: 20 minutes | Serves 2

Kcal 281, Carbs 2g/0.07oz, Fats17g/0.6oz, Protein 35g/1.23oz, Fiber 1g/0.03oz

Ingredients

- 370g/13oz of firm tofu
- 17g/1 tablespoon of nutritional yeast
- 1g/¼ a teaspoon of Turmeric
- Pepper and salt
- 180ml/¾ a cup of unsweetened almond milk
- 17g/1 tablespoon of chopped fresh chives

Preparation

1. Break the tofu into fairly large pieces in a large nonstick pan. Not any smaller than a mouthful, they break further while cooking.

2. Put in some turmeric and nutritional yeast combine carefully before cooking for a period of 5 minutes.

3. Pour in almond milk and simmer over medium heat for 10 minutes. Keep stirring occasionally till it softens into a creamy paste.

4. Add pepper and salt and top with some chives.

Lunch: Greek Quesadillas (See page 49)

Dinner: Pasta and Basil Tapenade (See page 65)

84 | TONY A. MORGAN

Day 11

Breakfast: Greek Omelet Casserole (See page 29)

Lunch: Grilled Garden Veggie Pizza

Kcal 349, Carbs 30.9g/1.08oz, Fat 25.6g/0.9oz, Protein 10.9g/0.40oz, Fiber 6g/0.2oz

Ingredients

- 40g/⅓ a cup of torn fresh basil
- 1 medium red onion
  sliced crosswise
- 240g/2 cups of shredded, divided
  part-skim mozzarella cheese
- 1 large sweet red pepper halved
- 50g/3 tablespoons of
  roasted minced garlic
- A small zucchini cut lengthwise
- 1 prebaked thin pizza crust
- 1 yellow summer squash
- 30ml/2 tablespoons of olive oil
- A pinch of pepper
- 2g/½ a teaspoon of salt

Preparation

1. Lightly coat the veggies with oil before sprinkling with some pepper and salt.

2. Grill the veggies while covered. For the onions and pepper, cook for 5 minutes each side till tender while the squashes and zucchini should take approximately 3 minutes to bake per side.

3. Separate the onions to form rings, slice the pepper into thin strips.

4. Lay the pizza crust flat then spread garlic atop before sprinkling with half the cheese on top.

5. Put the grilled veggies over the cheese and top with the remainder of the cheese.

6. Grill the pizza while covered for 7 minutes until the crust gets golden brown and all the cheese has melted.

7. Garnish with basil then serve.

Dinner: Pasta and Basil Tapenade (See page 65)

Day 12

Breakfast: The Greek Sushi Salad (See page 33)

Lunch: Mediterranean Herb Shrimp with Penne (See page 51)

Dinner: Asparagus Ham Dinner

Time: 30 minutes | Servings 3

Kcal 204, Carbs 29g/1.02oz, Fats 5g/0.17oz, Proteins 12g/0.42oz, Fiber 3g/0.1oz

Ingredients

- 🍽 30g/¼ a cup of shredded parmesan cheese
- 🍽 2 cups of uncooked pasta
- 🍽 A pinch of cayenne pepper
- 🍽 330g/¾ lb of fresh asparagus
- 🍽 2g/½ a teaspoon of dried basil
- 🍽 1 medium sweet yellow pepper
- 🍽 2g/½ a teaspoon of dried oregano
- 🍽 15ml/1 tablespoon of olive oil
- 🍽 2g/½ a teaspoon of salt
- 🍽 6 diced medium tomatoes
- 🍽 30g/¼ a cup of minced fresh basil
- 🍽 170g/6oz of boneless fully cooked ham

Preparation

1. Prepare and cook the pasta in accordance with the direction of the package.
2. Using a cast-iron skillet, quickly sauté the yellow pepper and the asparagus until tender.
3. Now put in tomatoes and ham.
4. Drain the cooked pasta and add to the asparagus mixture.
5. Mix in the fresh parsley before finishing off with the cheese.

Day 13

Breakfast: Oven-baked Rutabaga Wedges

Time: 20 minutes | Serves 4

Kcal 167, Carbs 7g/0.24oz, Fats 14g/0.5oz, Proteins 1g/0.03oz, Fibers1g/0.01oz

Ingredients

- 450g/1 lb rutabaga
- 60ml/¼ a cup olive oil
- Pepper and salt
- 4g/1 teaspoon chili powder

Preparation

1. Allow the oven to heat to a temperature of 200°C/400°F.
2. Rinse before peeling the rutabaga.
3. Slice into wedges and spread evenly on the baking sheet.
4. Add some pepper and salt before topping with some olive oil.
5. Bake in the oven for 20 minutes till the rutabaga wedges get that nice color.

Lunch: Mediterranean Salad with Balsamic Chicken (See page 52)

Dinner: The Mediterranean Chopped Salad (See page 68)

Day 14

Breakfast: The Greek Sushi Salad (See page 33)

Lunch: Terrific Turkey Meat Loaf
Time: 1 hour 5 minutes | Servings 4
Kcal 226, Carbs 14g/0.49oz, Fats 10g/0.35oz, Proteins 25g/0.88oz, Fiber 3g/0.1oz

Ingredients

- 450g/1 lb ground turkey
- 1 lightly beaten egg white
- 1g/¼ a teaspoon of pepper
- 60g/½ a cup of oat bran
- 1g/¼ a teaspoon of rubbed sage
- 60g/½ a cup of chopped green pepper
- 1g/¼ a teaspoon of dried marjoram
- 30g/¼ a cup of finely chopped onions
- 1g/¼ a teaspoon of celery salt
- 45ml/3 tablespoons of ketchup
- 2g/½ a teaspoon of Dijon mustard
- 34g/2 tablespoons of chopped ripe olives
- 1 minced garlic clove
- 15ml/1 tablespoon of Worcestershire sauce

Preparation

1. Bring the oven to a temperature of 162°C/375°F.

2. Using a large mixing bowl, mix every ingredient but the ground turkey for now.

3. Add the turkey to the mixture and mix it through.

4. Put into a rectangular sized baking tin pre-coated with cooking spray to make the loaves.

5. Cook in the oven for 50 minutes or until the internal temperature gets to 73°C/165°F.

6. Allow cooking before you serve.

Dinner: Mediterranean Stuffed Sweet Potatoes with Chickpeas and Avocado Tahini (See page 55)

Day 15

Breakfast: Banana Split Yogurt (See page 34)

Lunch: The Israeli Pasta Salad (See page 36)

Dinner: Blackened Catfish with Mango Avocado Salsa

Time: 30 minutes | Servings 4

Kcal 375, Carbs 17g/0.59oz, Fats 22g/0.77oz, Proteins 28g/0.98oz, Fiber 6g/0.21oz

Ingredients

- 10ml/2 teaspoons of olive oil
- 8g/2 teaspoons of dried oregano
- 30ml/2 tablespoons of lime juice
- 8g/2 teaspoons of ground cumin
- 34g/2 tablespoons of minced fresh cilantro
- 8g/2 teaspoons of paprika
- 40g/⅓ a cup of finely chopped onions
- 2g/½ a teaspoon of divided pepper
- 1 medium cubed avocado
- 4g/1 teaspoon of salt
- 1 medium cubed ripe mango
- 4 catfish fillets

Preparation

1. In a small mixing bowl, combine the paprika, cumin, oregano, salt, and half of the pepper and mix.

2. Coat the fish fillets with this mixture before refrigerating for 30 minutes.

3. In another separate mixing bowl, combine the cilantro, onion, avocado, mango dices, lime juice, salt, and the remainder of the pepper then chill in the fridge until serving.

4. Bring the oil to heat in a large skillet before cooking the marinated fillets until they get tender to the fork.

5. Serve with the salsa on the side.

Day 16

Breakfast: Low-carb Zucchini Nacho Chips

Time: 25 minutes | Serves 4

Kcal 145, Carbs 2g/0.06oz, Fats 14g/0.49oz, Proteins 1g/0.03oz, Fiber 1g/0.035oz

Ingredients

- A pinch of salt
- 375ml/1½ cups of coconut oil
- 15ml/1 tablespoon of Tex-Mex seasoning
- Large zucchini

Preparation

1. Using a Mandolin, chop the zucchini into round thin slices.
2. Put the slices in a colander and season with lots of salt and allow to settle for 5 minutes before squeezing out all the water.
3. Bring the oil up to 180°C/350°F in a skillet and fry the zucchini pieces in the hot oil.
4. Put in a paper towel to get rid of excess oil.
5. Add some taco seasoning and there you go!

Lunch: Cauliflower Pizza and Grilled Vegetables with Greek-Style Yogurt Pesto (See page 38)

Dinner: The Greek Goddess Bowl (See page 57)

Day 17

Breakfast: Quick and Easy Greek Salad (See page 24)

Lunch: Greek Pork Chops

Time: 25 minutes | Servings 4

Kcal 193, Carbs 2g/0.07oz, Fats 10g/0.35oz, Proteins 22g/0.77oz, Fiber 1g/0.035oz

Ingredients

- 4 boneless pork loin chops
- 30ml/2 tablespoons of olive oil
- 2g/½ a teaspoon of ground mustard
- 20ml/4 teaspoons of lemon juice
- 4g/1 teaspoon of pepper
- 15ml/1 tablespoon Worcestershire sauce
- 4g/1 teaspoon of garlic powder
- 8g/2 tablespoons ground oregano
- 4g/1 teaspoon of onion powder
- 4g/1 teaspoon of salt

Preparation

1. Using a large mixing bowl, combine every ingredient except the pork loin chops then mix thoroughly.

2. Now put in the pork chops making sure they are well coated. Refrigerate overnight for the best effect.

3. Drain the chops after a night of marination and discard the marinade.

4. Go ahead and grill, under medium to high heat while covered.

5. You will know the loin is ready once the internal temperatures get to 62°C/145°F.

6. Allow it to cool before serving.

Dinner: Greek Zucchini and Walnut Salad (See page 59)

Day 18

Breakfast: Mediterranean Breakfast Scrambled Eggs (See page 25)

Lunch: Greek Farro Salad (See page 41)

Dinner: Crunchy Oven-Baked Tilapia

Time: 25 minutes | Servings 4

Kcal 186, Carbs 6g/0.21oz, Fats 3g/0.1oz, Proteins 33g/1.16oz, Fiber 0

Ingredients

- 34g/2 tablespoon of minced fresh cilantro
- 4 tilapia fillets
- Cooking spray
- 15ml/1 tablespoon of reduced-fat mayonnaise
- 60g/½ a cup of panko breadcrumbs
- 15ml/1 tablespoon lime juice
- A pinch of pepper
- 1g/¼ a teaspoon of grated lime zest
- A pinch of onion powder
- 2g/½ a teaspoon of salt

Preparation

1. Bring the oven to a temperature of 218°C/425°F.
2. Generously coat the baking sheet with cooking spray.
3. In a mixing bowl, combine every ingredient except the cilantro, fillets, and breadcrumbs and mix well.
4. Coat the fillets entirely with the mayo mixture before adding another layer of breadcrumbs and finishing off with a spray of oil.
5. For 20 minutes, cook the fillets in the oven till they get tender to the fork.
6. Garnish with cilantro then serve.

Day 19

Breakfast: Peanut Butter Smoothie

Time: 1 minute | Serves 1

Kcal 198, Carbs 8g/0.28oz, Fats 17g/0.6oz, Proteins 6g/0.21oz, Fiber 6g/0.21oz

Ingredients

- 17g/1 tablespoon of peanut butter
- 1 serving liquid stevia
- 125ml/½ a cup of almond milk
- 17g/1 tablespoon of cocoa powder
- 34g/2 tablespoons of powdered peanut butter
- ¼ a medium avocado
- ¼ a cup of ice

Preparation

1. Blend all the ingredients except ice in a food processor to a consistent composition.

2. You can add milk if it is too thick. Add extra peanut butter powder if it's too thin.

3. Serve with some ice and enjoy!

Lunch: One-Pot Greek Chicken and Lemon Rice (See page 43)

Dinner: Easy Salad with Chicken Skewers (Grilled) (See page 60)

Day 20

Breakfast: Mediterranean Breakfast Scrambled Eggs (See page 25)

Lunch: Easy Sausage Pasta Toss
Time: 35 minutes | Servings 5
Kcal 340, Carbs 44g/1.55oz, Fats 10g/0.35oz, Proteins 21g/0.74oz, Fiber 6g/0.21oz

Ingredients

- 60g/2¼oz can of drained ripe olives
- 230g/8oz of uncooked multigrain spaghetti
- 2 425g/15oz cans diced, drained, ad unsalted tomatoes
- 30g/¼ a cup of seasoned bread crumbs
- 1 minced garlic clove
- 340g/¾ lb chopped turkey sausage links

Preparation

1. Prepare the spaghetti according to the directions on the package and drain any excess fluids.
2. On a skillet, bring some oil to heat under medium temperatures before tossing in the breadcrumbs until fried then remove them from the pan.
3. Now put the sausage chunks in the pan, add some oil, and fry till they lose the pink color.
4. Stir in the minced garlic and let them cook together for a minute before tossing in the olives and tomatoes.
5. In the same pan with the mixture, pour in the spaghetti and mix well.
6. Top with the baked breadcrumbs then serve.

Dinner: Mediterranean Salmon Souvlaki Bowls (See page 62)

Day 21

Breakfast: Egg Breakfast with Ham (See page 26)

Lunch: The Mediterranean Vegan Salad (See page 45)

Dinner: Chicken Pesto Roll-Ups
Time: 45 minutes | Servings 4
Kcal 374, Cabs 7g/0.24oz, Fats 17g/0.59oz, Proteins 44g/1.55oz, Fiber 1g/0.035oz

Ingredients

- 🍽 4 slices of halved provolone cheese
- 🍽 4 skinless and boneless
  chicken breasts
- 🍽 450g/1 lb of medium fresh
  mushroom slices
- 🍽 ½ a cup of prepared pestos

Preparation

1. Bring the oven to a temperature of 180°C/350°F.

2. Using a mallet, pound the breasts into thin slices before spreading ½ the pestos atop.

3. Chop half of the mushroom slices coarsely before scattering the reminder into a pre-oiled baking dish.

4. Divide the chopped slices of mushroom into 4 and top each breast with equal amounts of mushroom and cheese slices.

5. Now roll the chicken breast slices and secure with a toothpick before placing each roll having the seam side facing down on the mushrooms on top of the tray.

6. For 20 minutes, bake in the oven till the chicken breasts lose the pink color.

7. Finally, bring your broiler to heat then top the rolls with the remainder of the cheese and pestos.

8. For 5 minutes broil till the cheese is completely melted and turns brown. Remove the toothpicks from codpieces and serve.

Day 22

Breakfast: Avocado Toast with Persimmon, Fennel, and Pomegranate

Time: 10 minutes | Servings 2

Kcal 377, Carbs 41.6g/1.46oz, Fats 22.6g/0.8oz, Proteins 7.1g/0.25oz, Fiber 1g/0.03oz

Ingredients

- 17g/1 tablespoon of goat cheese
- 1g/¼ a teaspoon of salt
- 3ml/½ a teaspoon of lime juice
- 1 avocado
- Persimmon, thinly sliced

- 34g/2 tablespoons of pomegranate seeds
- 10ml/2 teaspoon of honey
- Fennel Bulb, thinly sliced with a few fennel fronds
- 2 pieces of bread, already toasted

Preparation

1. Cut the avocado into half and scoop out the flesh into a bowl.
2. Afterward, add the lime juice, salt, and goat cheese and then mash lightly with a fork.
3. Move to spread the mashed avocado you have onto the toasted bread, taking care to divide it evenly between the two slices.
4. Top with some slices of fennel and persimmon.
5. Sprinkle with pomegranate seeds and fennel fronds.
6. Drizzle all with honey and then proceed to serve.

Lunch: Greek-Style Meatball with Tzatziki (See page 46)

Dinner: Pasta and Basil Tapenade (See page 65)

Day 23

Breakfast: Avocado Tomato Gouda Socca Pizza (See page 27)

Lunch: Greek Fish Bake

Time: 30 minutes | Servings 4

Kcal 246, Carbs 6g/0.21oz, Fats 12g/0.42oz, Proteins 29g/1.0oz, Fiber 2g/0.07oz

Ingredients

- 30g/¼ a cup of crumbled feta cheese
- 4 cod fillets
- 230g/8oz can of tomato sauce
- 10ml/2 tablespoons of olive oil
- 30g/¼ a cup of sliced pitted Greek olives
- 1g/¼ a teaspoon of salt
- ½ thinly sliced red onion
- A pinch of pepper
- A small green pepper sliced into thin strips

Preparation

1. Bring the oven to a temperature of 204°C/400°F.
2. Generously coat the insides of a baking dish with oil before placing the cod slices atop.
3. Give the cod pieces a brush of oil, then sprinkle with some pepper and salt.
4. Go ahead and top with olives onions and green pepper.
5. Now, empty the tomato sauce over the codes before topping with the feta cheese.
6. Cook in the oven for 20 minutes until the cod fillets get tender to the fork.

Dinner: Roasted Herb Salmon (See page 64)

Day 24

Breakfast: Cauliflower Fritters with Hummus (See page 30)

Lunch: The Mediterranean Vegan Salad (See page 45)

Dinner: Italian Veggie Skillet

Time: 25 minutes | Servings 4

Kcal 342, Carbs 59g/2.08oz, Fats 4g/0.14oz, Proteins 16g/0.56oz, Fiber 11g/0.38oz

Ingredients

- Minced fresh basil
- 425g/15oz of unsalted garbanzo beans
- 30g/¼ a cup of parmesan cheese
- 425g/15oz of cannellini beans
- 250ml/1 cup of marinara sauce
- 425g/15oz of unsalted stewed tomatoes
- A pinch of red pepper flakes
- 250ml/1 cup of vegetable broth
- 4g/1 teaspoon of Italian seasoning
- 90g/¾ a cup of uncooked instant rice

Preparation

1. Using a large skillet put together every ingredient but the marinara sauce, basil, and grated cheese then allow them to boil under medium to high temperatures.

2. Once boiled, reduce the heat then cover the skillet and allow the rice to cook until tender.

3. Once the rice is done, mix in the marinara sauce and continuously stir until well combined before topping with the fresh basil and cheese.

Day 25

Breakfast: Blueberry Smoothie

Time: 5 minutes | Serves 1

Kcal 415, Carbs 10g/0.35oz, Fats 10g/0.35oz, Proteins 4g/0.14oz, Fiber 1g/0.03oz

Ingredients

- 205ml/7oz coconut milk
- 8ml/½ a tablespoon of lemon juice
- 32g/¼ a cup of blueberries
- 1g/¼ a teaspoon of vanilla extract

Preparation

1. Carefully blend all the ingredients to achieve a smooth texture.

Lunch: Greek Quesadillas (See page 49)

Dinner: Pasta and Basil Tapenade (See page 65)

Day 26

Breakfast: Egg Breakfast with Ham (See page 26)

Lunch: Feta Steak Tacos
Time: 30 minutes | Servings 8
Kcal 317, Carbs 25g/0.88oz, Fats 2g/0.07oz, Proteins 20g/0.7oz, Fiber 3g/0.1oz

Ingredients

- |●| Lime wedges
- |●| 450g/1 lb beef flat iron steak
  cut into thin slices
- |●| 30g/¼ a cup of crumbled
  garlic and herb feta cheese
- |●| 60ml/¼ a cup of Greek vinaigrette
- |●| 8 whole-wheat tortillas
- |●| 120ml/½ a cup of fat-free
  plain Greek yogurt
- |●| 30g/¼ a cup of sliced Greek olives
- |●| 10ml/2 teaspoons of lime juice
- |●| 30g/¼ a cup of sun-dried tomatoes
- |●| 15ml/1 tablespoon of oil
  from sundried tomatoes
- |●| Onion sliced into thin strips
- |●| 1 small green pepper cut into strips

Preparation

1. Put the beef slices into a large mixing bowl and pour in the vinaigrette. Allow the pieces to soak for 15 minutes.

2. Stir the lime juice and yogurt in a smaller bowl.

3. Using a good-sized skillet, bring the oil from sun-dried tomatoes to heat then add onions and pepper.

4. Cook till tender then transfers to a small bowl. Ass in the olives and sun-dried tomatoes.

5. Using the same pan, fry the beef slices until they lose the pink color.

6. To serve, put equal amounts of steak and the pepper mixture on each tortilla then top each with the crumbled cheese.

7. Each serving should be accompanied by the yogurt and lime mixture and a few pieces of the lemon wedges.

Dinner: Mediterranean Flatbread Pizza (See page 66)

Day 27

Breakfast: Banana Split Yogurt (See page 34)

Lunch: Mediterranean Herb Shrimp with Penne (See page 51)

Dinner: Avocado and Radish Salad with Fennel and Carrots

Time: 45 minutes | Serves 2

Kcal, Carbs 18g/0.63oz, Proteins 15g/0.53oz, Fats 43g/1.5oz, Fiber 18g/0.63oz

Ingredients

- An avocado
- 1 bulb fresh fennel
- Ground black pepper
- 2 carrots
- 30ml/2 tablespoons of olive oil
- 57g/2oz of leafy greens
- 57g/2oz of sesame seeds
- 75ml/5 tablespoons of tamari soy sauce
- 170g/6oz of radishes

Preparation

1. Bring the oven to a temperature of 180°C/350°F then line with a baking sheet with parchment paper.

2. Put sesame seeds in the sauce to marinate for about 15 minutes.

3. Bake the marinated seeds for 6-10 minutes. Remember sesame seeds.

4. Peel, pit, and dice the avocado into a bowl then combine with chopped carrots, radishes, and fennel.

5. Add some leafy green toppings before seasoning with pepper and generous amounts of olive oil.

6. Serve with baked sesame seeds.

Day 28

Breakfast: Bulgur Salad with Marinated Feta

Time: 12 hours 10 minute | Serves 4

Kcal 233, Carbs 2.9g/0.1oz, Fats 5.6g/0.19oz, Proteins 5.8g/0.2oz, Fiber 1g/0.03oz

Ingredients

For Marinated Feta

- 5g/1 teaspoon of lemon zest
- 60ml/½ a cup feta, cut into halves
- 4g/1 teaspoon of finely chopped fresh oregano leaves
- 4g/1 teaspoon of coarsely ground black pepper
- Olive oil
- 2g/½ a teaspoon of garlic powder

For the bulgur salad

- 375ml/1½ cup of boiling water
- 60ml/¼ a cup of minced fresh parsley
- 1 cucumber, with seeds already removed with a spoon and diced properly
- 60g/½ a cup of diced tomato
- 128g/1 cup of bulgur wheat
- 32g/¼ a cup of minced fresh mint leaves
- 30ml/2 tablespoons of lemon juice
- Salt
- Whole mint leaves to garnish

Preparation

1. For the marinated feta, place the feta in a suitable bowl and then add oregano and lemon zest; season with black pepper and garlic powder.

2. Transfer the mixture you have to a jar or a Tupperware with a lid.

3. Cover the cheese with olive oil and then cover the container and refrigerate for at least 12 hours.

4. For the bulgur salad, place the bulgur in a bowl and cover with boiling water.

5. Stir it quickly and allow it to sit at about room temperature for some minutes until it has softened slightly.

6. Strain it of any liquid that may be remaining.

7. Then mix in the chopped tomato, lemon juice, parsley, mint, chopped cucumber, and then season it all with salt to taste.

8. Serve almost immediately with marinated feta.

Lunch: Mediterranean Salad with Balsamic Chicken (See page 52)

Dinner: Roasted Vegetable Mediterranean-Style (See page 69)

Printed in Great Britain
by Amazon